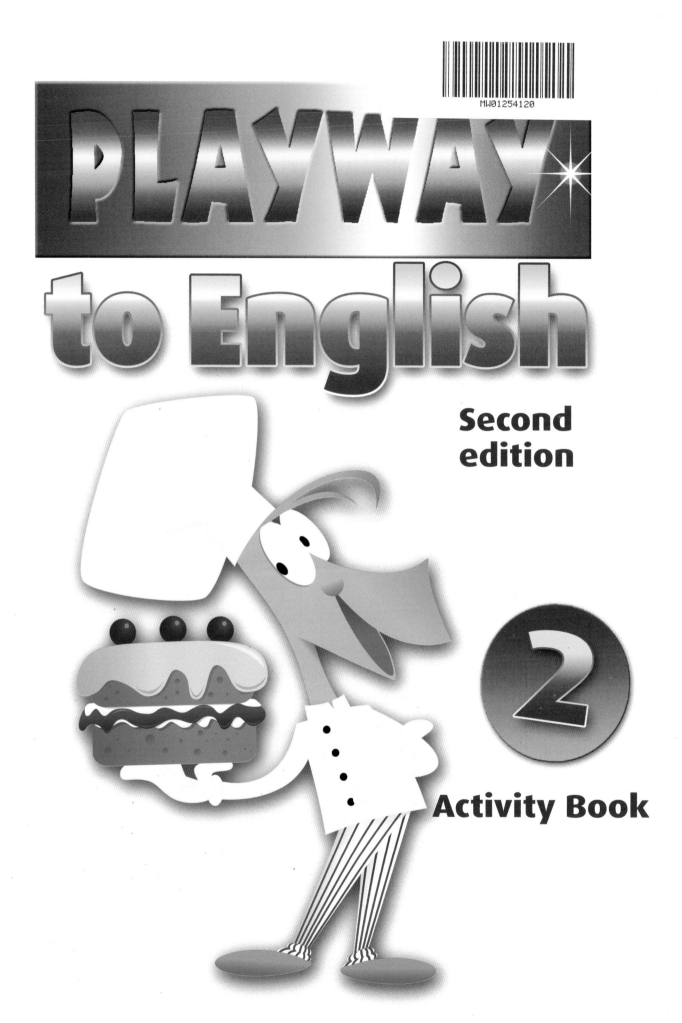

PLAYWAY to English

Second edition

2

Activity Book

Günter Gerngross • Herbert Puchta

Contents

Unit 6: Let's count

Structures
I'm so sorry.
Let's go to the (swimming pool).
Can I try?
(Ben) is thinking.
My favourite number is (seventy-two).

Vocabulary
twenty, thirty, forty, fifty, sixty, seventy, eighty, ninety, a hundred

Unit 7: Family

Structures
Swim across the river.
That's good. Yummy.
He's/We're happy.
Let's help him.
There are (five) (blue) T-shirts on the (cupboard).
In my family there's my mum ...

Vocabulary
mum, dad, brother, sister, grandpa, grandma

Unit 8: On the farm

Structures
Look for the cat.
Call the cat.
Feed the cat.
Put on your trainers.
Pick up your trainers.
Go outside.
There are (four) (dogs).
There's one (duck).
Who are you?
Hens lay eggs.
Everybody loves you.
On my farm there are ...

Vocabulary
cow, sheep, horse, pig, duck, cat, dog, mouse, hen, butterflies, bee, mouse

Unit 9: Travelling

Structures
A (bike) turning (left).
I get to school by (car).
I walk to school.
Put some (pears) in your basket.
Put it on your bike.

Vocabulary
left, right, underground, train, car, plane, bus

Unit 10: Holidays

Structures
Take off your (T-shirt).
Go to the (swimming pool).
Let's (be quiet).
I'm bored.
My favourite holiday ...

Vocabulary
cool off, jump in, build a sandcastle, go sailing, go fishing, go to the show

Hello again

1 **Listen and write the numbers.**

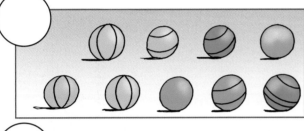

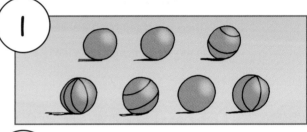

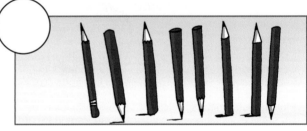

2 **Match the sentences to the pictures.**

Three white dogs.

Five blue planes.

Seven orange balls.

Ten green pencils.

Eight pink pencils.

Four red planes.

Two black dogs.

Nine green balls.

3 **Listen and colour.**

Let's eat the melon.

Where are the grapes?

Where's the melon?

£2, please.

4 **Read, match and colour.**

5 CD 1 / 8 **Listen and write the numbers.**

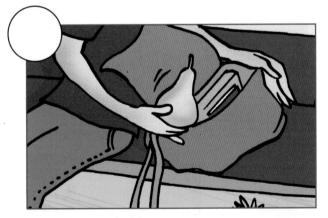

Listen and draw.

Maria

Andy

Tom

Sandra

Karen

Bob

Max

Benny

1

7 13 CD 1 **Listen and match.**

① ② ③ ④ ⑤ ⑥ ⑦ ⑧ ⑨ ⑩

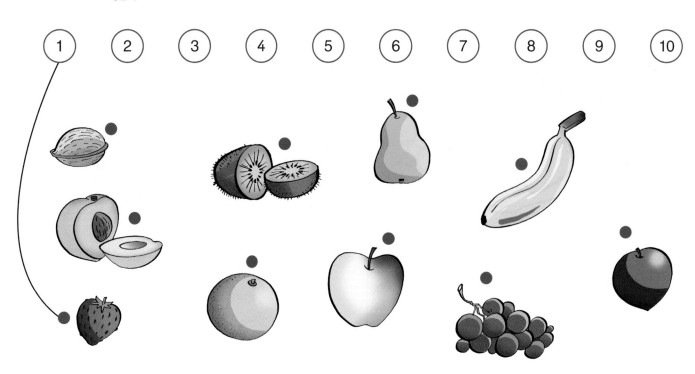

8 **Match the words to the pictures.**

◯ kiwi ◯ apple ◯ plum ◯ banana ◯ grapes

◯ nut ◯ peach ◯ pear (|) strawberry ◯ orange

9 **Find the six words.** ↓ →

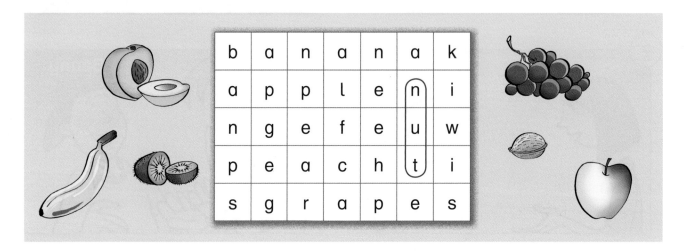

b	a	n	a	n	a	k
a	p	p	l	e	n	i
n	g	e	f	e	u	w
p	e	a	c	h	t	i
s	g	r	a	p	e	s

10   **Listen and circle.**

11 **Draw and say.**

Shopping

1 Match the words to the pictures.

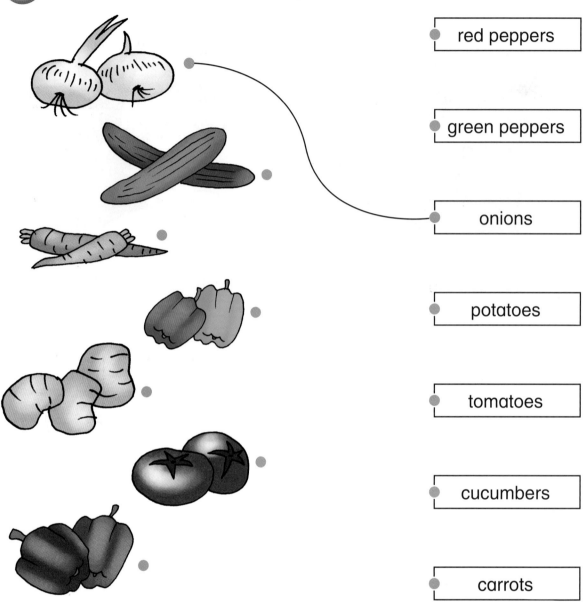

red peppers

green peppers

onions

potatoes

tomatoes

cucumbers

carrots

2 Write.

rsorcat **carrots**

soonni _____

sperppe _____

buccumesr _____

setotamo _____

sattopoe _____

3 **Look, read and write the numbers.**

①

②

③

④

◯ There's one onion, there are four cucumbers, four tomatoes, six carrots and three green peppers.

◯ There's one cucumber, there are two onions, four tomatoes, six carrots and three red peppers.

I There are three cucumbers, two onions, four tomatoes, six carrots and three red peppers.

◯ There are three cucumbers, two potatoes, four tomatoes, six carrots and three green peppers.

  Listen and write the names.

20
CD 1

Amy   James   Lily   Harry

5 **Say.**

Amy's table is number …

6 Look and write the numbers.

Thank you.

£2, please.

1 Mum, the cucumbers, please.

Goodbye.

Good morning.

Three onions, please.

7 **Look, count and write.**

3	4	5	6	7	8
three	four	five	six	seven	eight

2
two

9
nine

1
one

10
ten

🥒	🫑	🥕	🍅	🫑	🧅	🥔
7						

14

8   **Listen and circle.**

9 **Draw and say.**

My favourite fruit salad

In my favourite fruit salad there are _____

and _____ .

_____

1 **Colour and say.**

A

B

2 

31
CD 1

Listen and say.

1

2

3
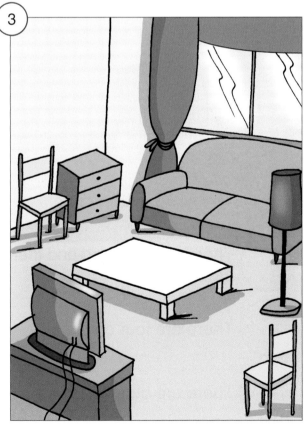

4

3 Match the sentences to the pictures.

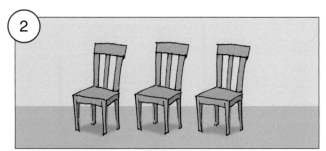

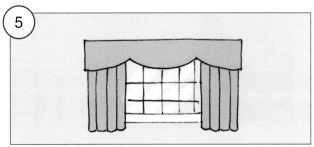
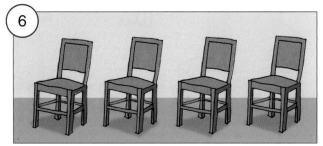

There's a cupboard and a lamp.

There's a blue sofa and a yellow sofa.

There are two sofas. A pink sofa and a yellow sofa. **1**

There are three chairs.

There are yellow curtains.

There's a cupboard and there are two lamps.

There are four chairs.

There are blue curtains.

4   Listen and write the numbers.

5 Do sums and write.

| ten | eleven | twelve | thirteen | fourteen | fifteen |
| sixteen | seventeen | eighteen | nineteen | twenty |

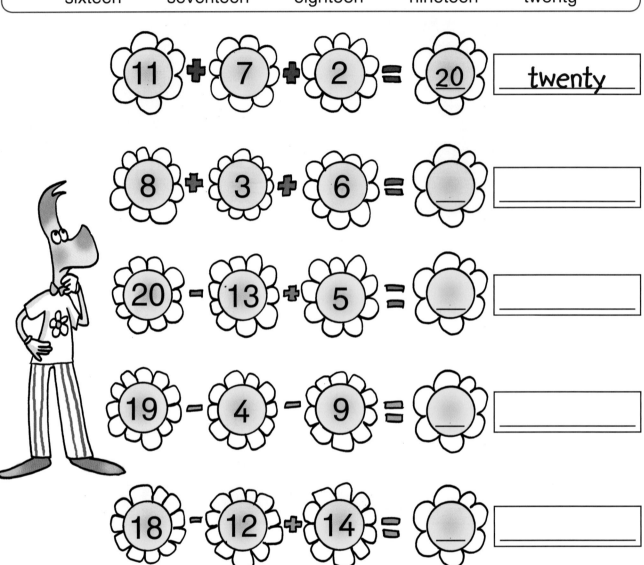

11 + 7 + 2 = 20   _twenty_

8 + 3 + 6 = ___

20 - 13 + 5 = ___

19 - 4 - 9 = ___

18 - 12 + 14 = ___

6 Write.

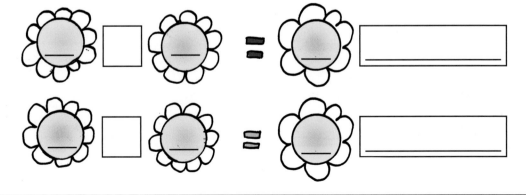

7 **Listen and match.**

8 **Draw and say.**

My crazy room

There's a _____ on the _____ .

There's a _____ on the _____ .

There's a _____ on the _____ .

And there's a _____ on the _____ .

_____

My body

Unit
4

1   Listen and write the numbers.

4
CD 2

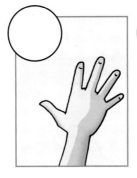

1

_____   _____   _____   head   _____

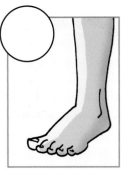

_____   _____   _____   _____   _____

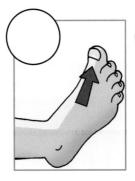

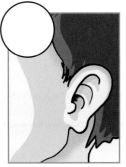

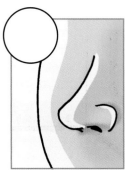

_____   _____   _____   _____   _____

2 Look at the pictures in 1 and write.

foot	finger	leg	hair
mouth	ear		
arm	toe	nose	eye
	hand		
head	tooth	shoulder	knee

22

3 **Listen and write the numbers.**

4  7 CD 2 **Listen and point.**

1

2

3

4

5

6

5 8 CD 2 **Listen again and write.**

| bed | Sam | hello | dog | no | and |

1. Sam gets out of _____ *bed* _____ .

2. He says _____ to his dog.

3. Oh, _____ !

4. _____ runs into the kitchen.

5. He brings his _____ some water.

6. Sam _____ his dog are happy.

6 Listen and colour.

I've got an idea.	Where are we going?
Look at my tooth.	Ouch, my back!
Next, please.	Watch me, Megan.

7 Read, match and colour.

8 Circle the words.

head mouth foot eye ear hand arm tooth nose toe leg finger knee hair shoulder

9 🎧 12 CD 2 Listen and circle.

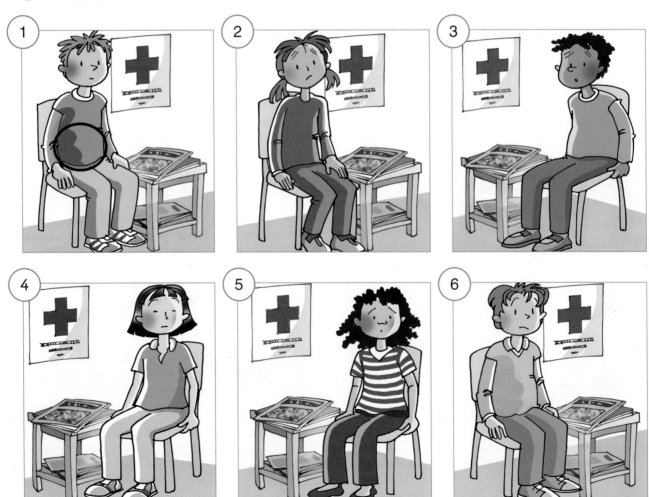

1

2

3

4

5

6

---

10 **Listen and draw.**

11 **Draw and say.**

My monster has got …

1 Find the ten words. ↓ →

s	o	t	s	h	i	r	t
j	a	c	k	e	t	d	f
t	r	a	i	n	e	r	s
x	w	p	r	a	b	e	o
q	h	a	t	v	r	s	c
u	p	j	e	a	n	s	k
l	k	c	s	h	o	e	s

2 🔘 17 CD 2 Listen and write the names.

Frank	Mike	Debra	Susan

_____   _____   _____

_____   _____   _____

3  **Listen and write the numbers.**

1

4 🔘 22 CD 2 **Listen and circle.**

5 👫 **Colour and say.**

A B

6 **Listen and write the numbers.**

7 🔊 27 CD 2 **Listen and colour.**

I don't like it.	Can I try the T-shirt on?
Can I help you?	I'll take the blue jacket.
That's nice.	Yellow?

8 **Read, match and colour.**

9  **Listen and colour.**

28
CD 2

10 **Draw, write and say.**

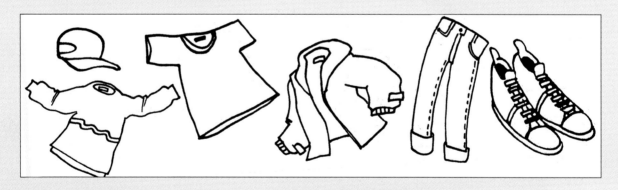

My favourite _____ is _____ .

My favourite _____ is _____ .

My favourite _____ is _____ .

My favourite _____ are _____ .

And my favourite _____ are _____ .

Let's count

1 31 CD 2 **Listen and write the numbers.**

70

2 **Match the numbers with the words. Colour.**

| fifty | twenty | thirty |

| seventy | ten | a hundred |

| sixty | forty | ninety | eighty |

3 **Listen and draw lines.**

4 **Find the ten numbers.** ↓ →

60
40
100
70
80

t	t	e	s	e	v	e	n	t	y
h	t	o	x	d	s	i	x	t	y
i	w	a	h	u	n	d	r	e	d
r	e	e	i	g	h	t	y	n	k
t	n	f	o	r	t	y	i	n	e
y	t	v	n	i	n	e	t	y	n
a	y	j	c	l	f	i	f	t	y

30
90
50
20
10

5 **Write the words.**

10 __ten__

20 _____

30 _____

40 _____

50 _____

60 _____

70 _____

80 _____

90 _____

100 _____

6 36 CD 2 **Listen and write the numbers.**

7 **37** **CD 2** **Listen and colour.**

I'm so sorry.	Let's go to the swimming pool.
Tim is ill.	Ben is thinking.
Anne, come here.	Can I try?

8 **Read, match and colour.**

9 Match and write.

ears   curtains   pullover

chair   carrot   mouth   nose

shoes   T-shirt

grapes   hand   sofa

potato   table

jacket   cap   strawberry

eyes   tomato

cupboard

hand

10 **Look and write.**

Max's favourite numbers are _____.

11 **Match the numbers to the pictures.**

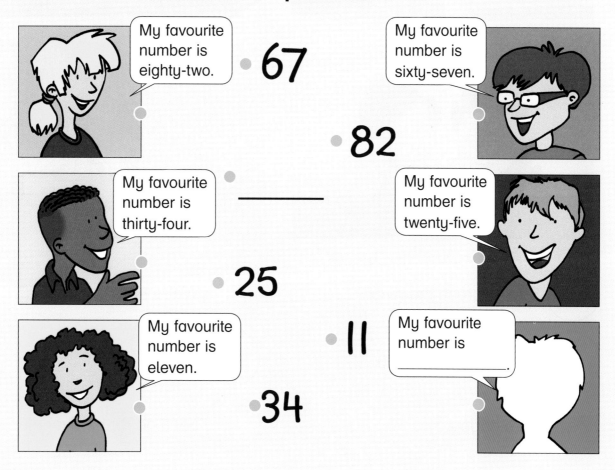

My favourite number is eighty-two.

67

My favourite number is sixty-seven.

82

My favourite number is thirty-four.

———

My favourite number is twenty-five.

25

My favourite number is eleven.

11

My favourite number is _____.

34

1 Look, read and match.

1

2

3

4

5

6

◯ Swim across the river.

◯ We're happy.

1 That's good. Yummy.

◯ Let's help him.

◯ He's happy.

◯ Let's go to the river.

2 CD 3   **Listen and write the numbers.**

3 Find the odd one out.

| cucumber | onion | plum | ~~glue~~ | carrot |

| peach | boat | banana | orange | apple |

| chair | table | cupboard | sofa | train |

| river | socks | dress | trainers | cap |

| hair | mouth | eyes | yellow | fingers |

| sixteen | one | nose | three | eighty |

4 How many sentences can you make?

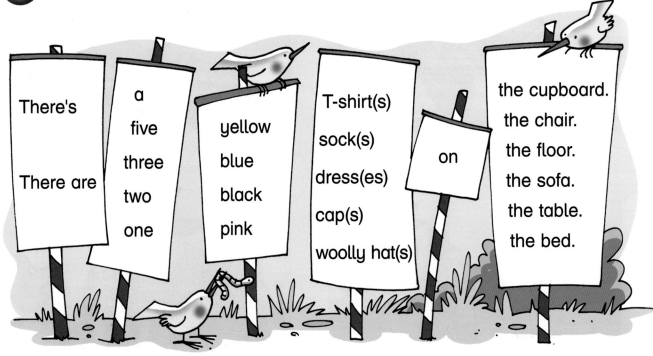

There's / There are

a / five / three / two / one

yellow / blue / black / pink

T-shirt(s) / sock(s) / dress(es) / cap(s) / woolly hat(s)

on

the cupboard. / the chair. / the floor. / the sofa. / the table. / the bed.

5 Look, read and write the names.

Oliver

Hi, I'm Laura.
In my family there's my mum, my dad, my two brothers and my grandpa.

Hi, I'm Jason.
In my family there's my mum, my dad, my two brothers and my grandma.

Hi, I'm Natalie.
In my family there's my mum, my two sisters, my grandpa and my grandma.

Hi, I'm Oliver.
In my family there's my mum, my dad, my two sisters and my grandma.

6  CD 3 9 **Listen and point.**

1

2

3

4

5

6

7 **Match the sentences to the pictures.**

( ) Do you like the yellow bird?

( ) Oh no, my curtains!

( ) It's from your bedroom.

( ) Yes, thank you.
It's wonderful.

(1) Here you are, Grandma.

( ) Thank you, Ryan.

8 **Look and say.**

In my family there's my mum, my dad, my brother Ronnie and me.

9 **Draw and say.**

In my family there's ...

On the farm

1
12
CD 3
Listen and write the numbers.

_____

I

Pick up your trainers. _____ _____

2 **Look at the pictures in** **1** **and write.**

Feed the cat.   Put on your trainers.

Look for the cat.

Pick up your trainers.   Go outside.

Call the cat.

3 **Find the ten names of the animals.** ↓ →

c	o	w	c	s	h	e	e	p
s	r	t	a	m	o	u	s	e
b	u	t	t	e	r	f	l	y
e	d	u	c	k	s	p	i	g
e	d	o	g	h	e	n	f	l

4 **Read. Tick the correct pieces to make a sentence (✓).**

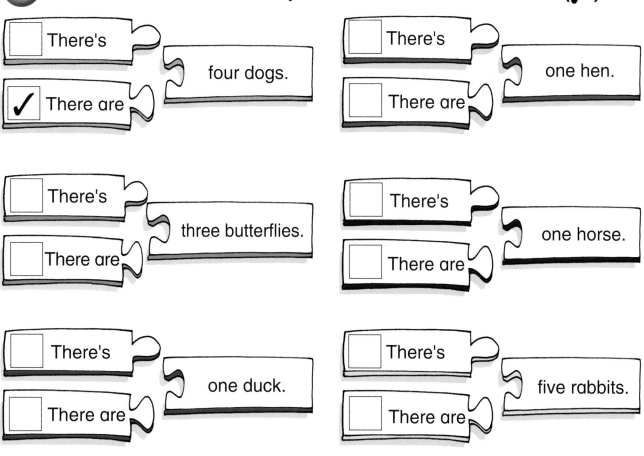

☐ There's

✓ There are   four dogs.

☐ There's

☐ There are   one hen.

☐ There's

☐ There are   three butterflies.

☐ There's

☐ There are   one horse.

☐ There's

☐ There are   one duck.

☐ There's

☐ There are   five rabbits.

5 Look, read and match.

( ) Who are you?

( ) Eddie is sad.

( ) Eddie is happy.

( ) Hens lay eggs.

(I) Bees make honey.

( ) Everybody loves you.

6 **Look and write.**

A

B

1
In picture A there are ____three____ ducks.

In picture B there are two ducks.

2
In picture A there's a white hen.

In picture B there's a _____ hen.

3
In picture A there are six sheep.

In picture B there are just _____ .

4
In picture A there's a black horse.

In picture B there's a _____ horse.

5
In picture A there are _____ cows. In picture B there are five.

6
In picture A there are three cats. In picture B there are

just _____ cats, the _____ cat is missing.

7 Read and match.

1 Who are you? ━━━━━━━━━━━ It's blue.

2 Happy birthday! ━━━━━━━━━━━ I'm Eddie.

3 What colour is your cap? • • Thank you.

4 Do you like roses? • • An apple.

5 What's in your room? • • Yes, they smell wonderful.

6 What is it? • • A pink sofa.

8 Look, read and complete.

1 What do 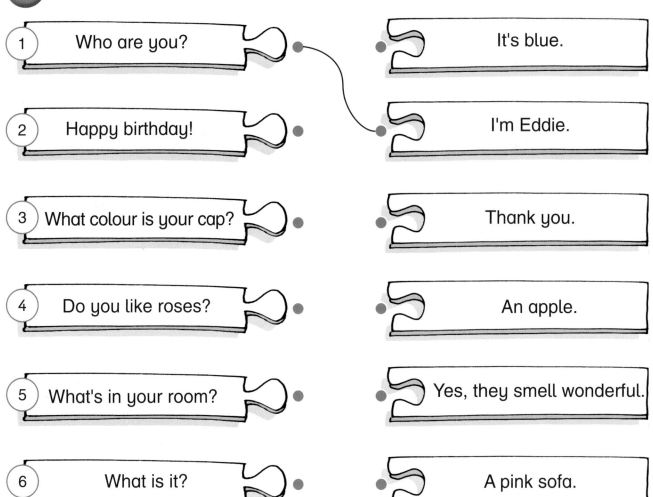 C O W S make? – They make milk.

2 Who makes 🍯 _ _ _ _ _ _ ? – Bees.

3 Do 🐔 _ _ _ _ _ lay 🥚 _ _ _ _ _ ? – Yes, they do.

4 Do you like my 🌸 _ _ _ _ _ _ _ _ _ _ ? – Yes, they smell wonderful.

5 What do 🐛 _ _ _ _ _ _ _ _ _ _ _ _ _ eat? – They eat old leaves.

9 **Look and read.**

On my farm there are six horses, five sheep, two cows, four ducks and there's one hen.

10 **Draw, write and say.**

On my farm there are ...

_____

_____

1 **Look and write.**

A car turning right.

_____

_____

_____

_____

_____

2 Listen and write the names.

CD 3

| Ella | Tom | ~~Polly~~ | Patrick | Mia | Ken |

_____

_____

_____

Polly

_____

_____

_____

3 24 CD 3 **Listen and write the numbers.**

(|)

4 **Match the sentences to the pictures.**

( ) What a heavy basket.

( ) What a strong wind!

( ) Nicole goes by bus.

( ) Can I have an apple?

( ) What's in your basket?

(|) It starts raining.

5 Find the odd one out.

| peach | ~~onion~~ | plum | orange | banana |

| train | boat | plane | bus | basket |

| hat | T-shirt | jacket | shoes | pencil |

| eggs | legs | teeth | hands | feet |

6 Look and write.

 Paul

 Melissa

 Mike

 Caroline

Paul: I get to school by ___train___ .

Melissa: I _____ .

Mike: I _____ .

Caroline: I _____ .

7 27 CD 3 **Listen and point.**

8 28 CD 3 **Listen again and write.**

| bike | train | pears | Oh, no | basket | left |

1) Put some _____ **pears** _____ in your basket.

2) Pick up the _____ .

3) Put it on your _____ .

4) Turn _____ into the station.

5) Get on the _____ .

6) _____ ! Where's your basket?

9 **Look and read. Then draw and say.**

Holidays

1   Look and write.

A

B

1. In picture A there are three children.

   In picture B there are _____ **four** _____ children.

2. In picture A there's a _____ dog.

   In picture B there's a black and _____ dog.

3. In picture A there are _____ bikes.

   In picture B there are four.

4. In picture A Pam is wearing yellow trainers.

   In picture B she is wearing _____ trainers.

6. In picture A there's one ball.

   In picture B there are _____ balls.

2  **Listen and point.**

33
CD 3

3 **Match the sentences to the pictures.**

◯ Jump in.

◯ Take off your jeans and T-shirt.

◯ Go to the swimming pool.

◯ Swim.

(1) You're hot.

◯ Cool off.

4 Look and write.

Let's jump in.   Too late.   It's asleep.
    Look at its big teeth.   Let's be quiet.   Careful!

Let's be quiet.

_____

_____

_____

_____

_____

5  **Listen and write the numbers.**

6 38 CD 3 **Listen and colour.**

| Let's build a sandcastle. | Let's go fishing. |

| Let's go home. | I'm bored. |

| Let's go sailing. | Let's go to the show. |

7 **Read, match and colour.**

8 **Look and read.**

My favourite holiday: at home with Benny and Linda.

9 **Draw, write and say.**

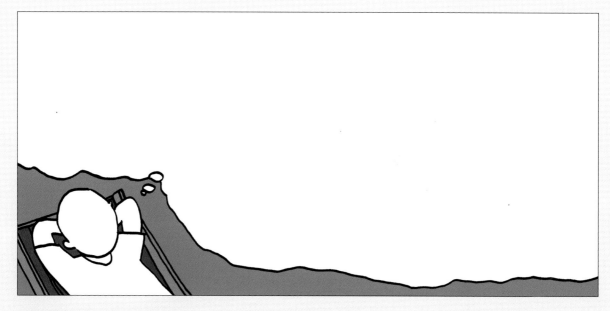

My favourite holiday

_____

_____

Acknowledgements:

The authors and publishers are grateful to the following illustrators:
Roberto Battestini, Pescara; Francesca Carabelli, Rome; Antje Hagemann, Berlin; Svjetlan Junaković, Zagreb; Nancy Meyers, Minneapolis; Mercè Orti, Barcelona

The authors and publishers would like to thank the following for permission to reproduce photographs:
Gerda Eicholzer p. 12 (b/children), iStockphoto.com pp. 12 (child: Amy/Aldo Murillo), 12 (child: James/Rich Legg), 12 (child: Lily/Jani Bryson), 12 (child: Harry/Maica), 55 (child: Paul/Steven Stone), 55 (child: Melissa/Robert Hunt), 55 (child: Mike/Chris Schmidt), 55 (child: Caroline/Rich Legg)

The publishers are grateful to the following contributors:
Andrew Oliver: cover design
Amanda Hockin: concept design
Hansjörg Magerle: book design and page make-up
Bill Ledger: cover illustration
James Richardson (The Soundhouse, London);
Daniel Richards (Daniel Networks, Milano, England): audio recordings
Lorenz Maierhofer: song writing
Herwig Burghard (TONBURG Tonstudio Burghard): music and arrangements; digital edit, sound-design and mastering

System Requirements:

Operating systems: Windows 2000, XP, Vista
CPU: Pentium 1 GHz
Memory: 256 MB RAM, (Vista: 512 MB RAM)
Graphics card: min. 800 x 600, 16 bit colour
CD-ROM drive: min. 16x speed
Sound card: full duplex, speakers or headphones

PLAYWAY

to English

Second edition

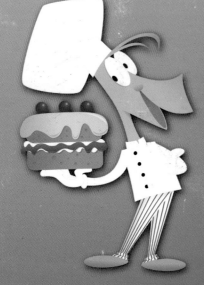

Playway to English Second edition is a new
version of the popular four-level course for
teaching English to young children.
Pupils acquire English through play, music and
Total Physical Response, providing them with a
fun and dynamic language learning experience.

In the Activity Book children can:

- Practise all the target language from the Pupil's Book
- Consolidate learning with an engaging CD-ROM,
  containing a rich assortment of exciting activities

CAMBRIDGE
UNIVERSITY PRESS
www.cambridge.org

ISBN 978-0-521-13114-8

9 780521 131148